Solar Eclipse

Lily Erlic

EYEDISCOVER

www.openlightbox.com

EYEDISCOVER

Go to **www.openlightbox.com** and enter this book's unique code.

BOOK CODE

AVR59749

EYEDISCOVER brings you optic readalongs that support active learning.

Published by Lightbox Learning Inc.
276 5th Avenue, Suite 704 #917
New York, NY 10001
Website: www.openlightbox.com

Library of Congress Control Number: 2023946973

ISBN 978-1-7911-5934-4 (hardcover)

Printed in Guangzhou, China
1 2 3 4 5 6 7 8 9 0 27 26 25 24 23

102023
102122

Project Coordinator: Priyanka Das
Art Director: Terry Paulhus
Layout: Jean Marie Faye Rodriguez

The publisher acknowledges Dreamstime, Getty Images, and Shutterstock as the primary image suppliers for this title.

EYEDISCOVER provides enriched content, optimized for tablet use, that supplements and complements this book. EYEDISCOVER books strive to create inspired learning and engage young minds in a total learning experience.

Your EYEDISCOVER Optic Readalongs come alive with...

Audio
Listen to the entire book read aloud.

Video
High resolution videos turn each spread into an optic readalong.

OPTIMIZED FOR
- ✓ TABLETS
- ✓ WHITEBOARDS
- ✓ COMPUTERS
- ✓ AND MUCH MORE!

This title is part of our EyeDiscover digital subscription

1-Year EyeDiscover Subscription
ISBN 978-1-4896-8346-5

Access all EyeDiscover titles with our digital subscription.
Sign up for a FREE trial at **www.openlightbox.com/trial**

The digital components of this book are guaranteed to stay active for at least five years from the date of publication.

Solar Eclipse

In this book, you will learn about

- what one is
- how it happens
- what one looks like

and much more!

A solar eclipse happens when the Moon blocks the Sun's light from reaching Earth.

In a solar eclipse, the Moon moves between Earth and the Sun. Its shadow falls on Earth.

A solar eclipse can be partial. This means that only some of the Sun is blocked by the Moon.

The Moon blocks the Sun completely in a total solar eclipse.

Total solar eclipses only happen about once every 18 months.

The next total solar eclipse will fall on April 8, 2024.

Solar eclipses can only be seen from certain places.

People in Mexico, the United States, and Canada will be able to see the April 8, 2024, solar eclipse.

Solar eclipses can hurt a person's eyes. People should only watch them using special glasses.

SOLAR ECLIPSES BY THE NUMBERS

Between **2001** and **2100**, there will have been **224** partial and total **solar eclipses**.

Scientists have been able to **predict** solar eclipses for more than **2,000 years**.

Solar eclipses can happen **between 2 and 5 times** in a **year.**

Solar **eclipse glasses** are **100,000 times darker** than regular sunglasses.

The **last time** that there were **5 solar eclipses** in **1 year** was in **1935.**

A total solar eclipse can **only be seen** in the **same spot** on Earth about **once every 375 years.**

KEY WORDS

Research has shown that as much as 65 percent of all written material published in English is made up of 300 words. These 300 words cannot be taught using pictures or learned by sounding them out. They must be recognized by sight. This book contains 36 common sight words to help young readers improve their reading fluency and comprehension. This book also teaches young readers several important content words, such as proper nouns. These words are paired with pictures to aid in learning and improve understanding.

Page	Sight Words First Appearance
5	a, Earth, from, light, the, when
6	and, between, in, its, moves, on
8	be, by, can, is, means, of, only, some, that, this
12	about, every, once
15	next, will
16	places
18	people, see, states, to
21	eyes, should, them, watch

Page	Content Words First Appearance
5	Moon, solar eclipse, Sun
6	shadow
11	total solar eclipse
12	months
15	April
18	Canada, Mexico, United States
21	glasses, person

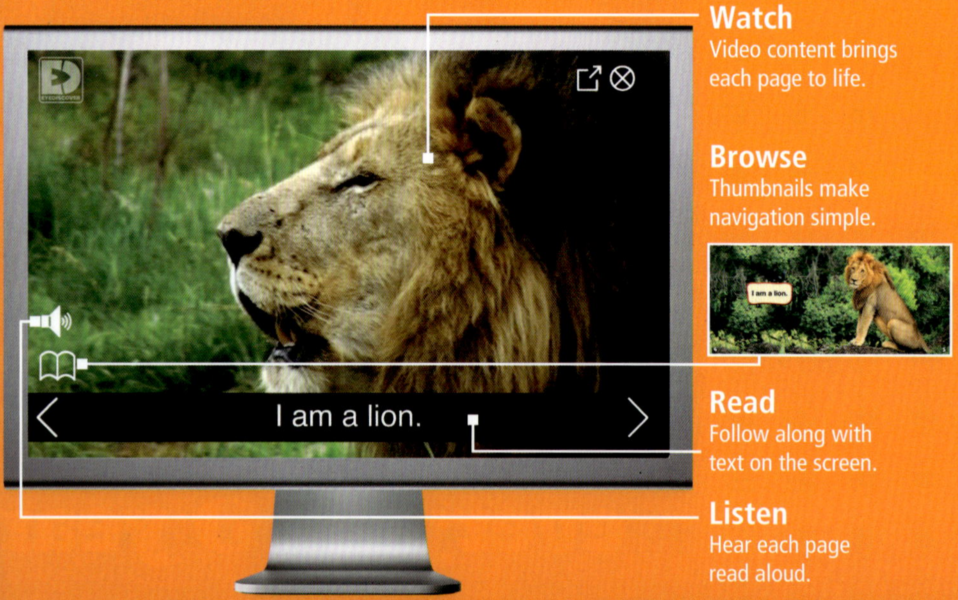

EYEDISCOVER

Go to www.openlightbox.com and enter this book's unique code.

BOOK CODE

AVR59749